Absolute Crime Presents:

Jeff Davis 8

*The True Story Behind the Unsolved Murder
That Allegedly Inspired Season One of True
Detective*

ABSOLUTE CRIME

By Fergus Mason

**Absolute Crime Books
www.absolutecrime.com**

Table of Contents

About Us

Absolute Crime publishes only the best true crime literature. Our focus is on the crimes that you've probably never heard of, but you are fascinated to read more about. With each engaging and gripping story, we try to let readers relive moments in history that some people have tried to forget.

Remember, our books are not meant for the faint at heart. We don't hold back—if a crime is bloody, we let the words splatter across the page so you can experience the crime in the most horrifying way!

If you enjoy this book, please visit our homepage to see other books we offer; if you have any feedback, we'd love to hear from you!

Introduction

If anyone is planning a book about rural Louisiana they should put a photo of Jefferson Davis Parish on the cover. Right on the edge of Cajun country, it's a low-lying area with a lot of water around. The eastern border of the county is formed by the Mermentau River and its tributary, the Bayou Nezpique. To the south lies Lake Arthur. Most of the parish is less than fifty feet above sea level and many of the fields are heavily irrigated for rice. Others have been dug out for crawfish ponds. The parish is home to just over 30,000 people, who're spread out over five incorporated towns - only one of which, parish seat Jennings, has more than 10,000 people – and scores of small settlements and farms. From Jennings it's a three-hour drive to either New Orleans or Houston along Interstate 10. The sole airport is just outside Jennings and can't handle anything much bigger than a Lear, and the only railway is the Union Pacific's freight line that runs right through Jennings. Louisiana's first oil well was drilled in the parish in 1901 but the basic economy has always been based on agriculture, and when oil production declined again the crops kept coming in. It's not a rich place – a fifth of the population is below the poverty line – but the people get by. Ethnically the population is pretty mixed, with Acadian, German and African-American origins dominating. Cajun French is still widely spoken, more so in the smaller settlements.

Jefferson Davis Parish has been described as quaint, and in many ways it certainly is. For anyone from a big city much of the area, especially out among the farms, is like a trip in a time machine. As for the name itself it doesn't date back to the Civil War; the place was named after the only president of the Confederate States of America in 1913, long after the fall of Richmond. That war passed out of living memory long ago and its legacy hasn't caused real problems for the parish, unlike many other places in the old South. To most of the residents the name is just a fact of life, and there hasn't been much pressure to change it. The quaintness shows in other ways; in the little white-painted wooden churches that form the center of most settlements, the elegant French colonial architecture that's still so common and the traditional way of life in the farming communities.

- X -

The modern world hasn't passed the parish by, of course, and sadly that applies to some of its nastier aspects too. Interstate 10 is a major route for drug dealers through the southern USA and Jennings has become one of their regular stops. That's created a market for crack cocaine in the town and wherever crack goes it brings problems with it. The homicide rate in the parish is 7.78 per 100,000 people each year,[i] which is well above the US average of 4.8, and a lot of those deaths are clustered in and around Jennings. On paper Jeff Davis is a much safer place to live than the state average – Louisiana's murder rate is 14.37 per 100,000 annually – but that's distorted by New Orleans, which rivals Detroit as the murder capital of the USA. For a sleepy rural community Jefferson Davis is a lot more violent than you'd expect, and these days cheap, potent rocks of cocaine are at the root of a lot of that violence.

Crack addicts are famously willing to do just about anything to subsidize their habit so street prostitution has become a real issue, mostly concentrated in the town's poorer neighborhoods south of the railway track. Prostitution – especially on the street – is a dangerous business, so the sheriff's office weren't too surprised when the first one turned up dead. As the body count climbed people started to take notice, but despite all their efforts the killings continued until eight women were dead.

With so many bodies and no solid evidence there was predictable anger in the community and not all of it was directed at the mysterious killer. It's common in high profile unsolved homicides for law enforcement to face criticism as the investigation drags on, but in the area around Jennings the public's feelings ran a lot deeper than that. They weren't just annoyed that the police couldn't stop the killings. They were worried that they might be committing them.

Chapter 1: The First Year

One of the things Louisiana is justly famous for is its Cajun cuisine, which is now popular pretty much everywhere in the western world, but the roots of that cuisine lie in the state's widespread and long-standing poverty. For many early Louisianans being able to cook up something edible from whatever you could hunt or catch wasn't a virtue – it was a necessity. A lot of people keep the tradition going, whether to stretch their income or because it's just the way they've always done things. Retiree Jerry Jackson had enough time on his hands to spend some of it fishing and if he could bring in something decent for the pan that was always a nice bonus. The muddy waters of the Grand Marais canal, just over three miles southwest of Jennings, could usually be relied on to give up a couple of catfish, and the concrete bridge on Highway 1126 made a perfect place to cast from. Silt had built up around the bridge supports, splitting the canal into two narrow channels, and mats of floating vegetation and debris tend to collect upstream of it; it's an ideal spot to find a scavenging catfish.

On May 20, 2005 Jerry was down at the bridge sorting out his line when he spotted a pale outline in the water. At first he thought it was a prank – some mannequins had been stolen from a local store a few days ago, and he guessed this was one of them caught among the rank grass. Then he caught a shimmer in the air above the shape and took a closer look. It was a swarm of flies, and mannequins don't draw flies. Alarmed, Jerry called 911. First deputies from the Jefferson Davis Parish Sheriff's Office arrived, then detectives from the Criminal Investigations Division. Carefully the detectives climbed down the bank, verifying what Jerry had thought – this was no plastic dummy, but the body of a petite woman with short, light brown hair. They took dozens of photographs then, when they were sure they'd recorded the location exactly, they set about getting the corpse out of the water. That wasn't a pleasant task. Water does nasty things to corpses, and in May the temperature in the parish climbs into at least the mid-80s most days. The body was decaying and unrecognizable, and there was nothing distinctive about the clothes – blue jeans, blue panties and a white blouse.

Of course there's one way to identify a corpse that works even when it's pretty decayed – fingerprints. Back at the morgue the body was printed, and the detectives' luck was in. They got a match, and they didn't even have to go on the wires to the state police or FBI to do it; their local files were enough. The dead woman was 28-year-old Loretta Lynn Chaisson Lewis and she had a record with the sheriff's office. A lot of it was standard troubled families stuff. Chaisson was separated from her husband and the split hadn't been amicable – they'd called local law enforcement on each other more than once. She also had links to the drug scene, though, and she was known to work as a prostitute in exchange for crack. Most days she was either walking the streets in south Jennings or hanging out at a notorious drug den waiting for an offer. She often vanished for a couple of days at a time without letting anyone know where she was going. With such a chaotic life it wasn't all that unusual that she hadn't been reported missing – one of the sad facts that makes street hookers so vulnerable. The last known sighting of her was on May 17, three days before her body was found.

At first it seemed like there was no great mystery to Chaisson's death. She was a known street prostitute and that's what sociologists call a high-risk lifestyle. She also had high levels of alcohol and cocaine in her system, two more risk factors. There was no hard evidence of homicide apart from the location of the body and a small patch of blood under her hair that might have come from a blow to the head, but apart from that it looked like the sort of depressingly familiar killing that law enforcement officers see all the time. That soon changed though. Inside a month it was clear the case wasn't going to be wrapped up so easily.

- X -

Ernestine Marie Daniels Patterson was a 30-year-old African-American from a large Jennings family – she had three brothers and six sisters. With two sons and two daughters she and husband Calvin Patterson had a decent-sized family themselves, but now they were separated and Ernestine had turned to prostitution to support a crack habit. A cheerful woman with sparkling eyes and a ready smile, Ernestine had worked in the Wendy's restaurant in Jennings and at the Iota State School until her drug problem got to be too much. By early 2005 she was spending most of her time selling herself at the Boudreaux Inn, a run-down motel that stands beside Highway 26 on the northern edge of Jennings. Then on June 16, 2005 she was reported missing.

It's not just fish Louisianans take from the waterways that crisscross their state. Crawfish, turtles, snakes and even alligators often find their way from the swamps and rivers to the pot, but one of the most popular catches is the bullfrog. Like their French ancestors Cajuns are partial to a plate of frogs' legs and the big bullfrog, which is very numerous in the state, is an ideal source. Froggers hunt in boats or along the banks of drainage ditches, sweeping the banks with powerful flashlights. When a frog's eyes reflect back at them they hold the animal in the beam, quieting it until they can grab it or nail it with a frog gig, a light four or five-tined spear. On the night of June 18 a group of froggers was hunting along a small canal beside Highway 102, about two miles south of Jennings, when they found more than they were expecting. Highlighted by the beams of their lights was the partly dressed corpse of a woman.

The body turned out to be Daniels and this time it was clear she was a murder victim – her throat had been cut. Apart from this obvious wound her corpse was seriously decomposed, to the point where investigators couldn't get enough body fluids to run a DNA check on her. There was no mistaking the gaping wound that had killed her, though. There were even potential suspects. The parish's farmers often hire seasonal labor, mostly from Mexico, and there was a group of these migrant workers in town around the time of her death. The news coming out of the sheriff's office was that they believed she had cheated the Mexicans and been killed in revenge. The source of this story seems to have been another local prostitute, LaConia "Muggy" Brown; she later told the sheriff's office that she heard the story at the San Francisco Grocery in Jennings.

That line of questioning didn't lead anywhere though and the next development was in April 2006, when local men Bryon Chad Jones and Lawrence Nixon were arrested and charged with second-degree murder.[ii] The key witness was Nixon's girlfriend, who claimed Daniels had been killed by Jones and Nixon and pointed out a porch where she said the body had been placed in a trash bag before being dumped. A vehicle was also identified as having been used to transport the body, but forensic examination of both the porch and car found nothing to back up the story. That left the girlfriend's testimony as the only evidence, and she wasn't claiming to have seen either the killing itself or Ernestine's body. Bryon Jones appeared in court on April 22 and pled not guilty; not long after he and Nixon were released and the case against them collapsed through lack of evidence.

The investigation also looked at Frankie Richard, a prominent figure in the local vice scene, and his niece Hannah Conner. Richard had known Loretta Chaisson but wasn't known to be associated with Daniels. No charges were laid against him, but his name would surface again and again as the death toll mounted.

By this point almost a year had passed since the two deaths and the picture was far from clear. Daniels was definitely a murder victim but the verdict on Chaisson was open; she had been prescribed medication for seizures about a year before she died, and her estranged husband still believes she may have stopped taking the tablets and died of a seizure.[iii] As 2006 passed with no more incidents the county's attention moved on, apart from the friends and families of the two dead women. Right now there was nothing to definitely connect the deaths. The fact they knew each other and were both part of the same scene could be coincidence; after all it's a dangerous scene. Early in 2007, however, any thoughts of coincidence would be wiped away for good.

Chapter 2: The Pace Picks Up

Frankie Richard claims he once ran a string of strip clubs in the Jennings area, but now he leads a quieter life. In 2007, at least, it wasn't a completely law abiding one; he's admitted to being a crack addict, he has a history of arrests for assault and he spent a lot of time hanging out with street hookers. On March 6, 2007 he was in a room he'd taken at the Budget Inn, 600 yards north of the Boudreaux Inn on Highway 26. The Budget Inn is slightly more upscale than the Boudreaux, although that's not saying much; it's a cluster of buildings with plenty of parking space and basic facilities. Now a year-old Chevy Silverado truck pulled into the parking lot and three young women got out. The truck belonged to Connie Siler. With her were 31-year-old Tracee Chaisson, Loretta Chaisson Lewis's cousin, and 21-year-old Kristen Gary Lopez. All three of them headed to Richard's room. In the two weeks he'd had it Tracee and Kristen had spent a lot of time there partying with him – he knew both of them, especially Kristen, well – but now, according to him, he accused them of trying to steal from him and threw them out of the room.

Kristen Lopez was well known around Jennings. She was short, thin and awkward looking, with a triangular face and prominent ears. She was also mentally disabled, severely enough that she'd taken part in the Baton Rouge Special Olympics when she was younger. Now she called Richard "Uncle Frankie" and hung around his house a lot. She also sold her body at the Boudreaux Inn and on the street to buy drugs. Now, after leaving Richard's motel room and climbing into the truck, she dropped out of sight. Tracee Chaisson reported Kristen missing on March 15. Three days later her nude body turned up in a canal just off Highway 99, fifteen miles southwest of Jennings. It was badly decomposed and the autopsy couldn't find any obvious signs of injuries that might have been caused before her death, although she'd been badly chewed by alligators after going into the canal.[iv] What they did find was that, like Chaisson and Daniels, her body was laced with alcohol and cocaine.

- X -

Whitnei Dubois had a life that adds whole new layers of meaning to the word "dysfunctional." Abandoned along with her brother and sister at six months old, she was fostered by a Jennings family for the next two years and had settled in well. Then her mother reappeared and demanded her back. Social Services tried to block the move but Whitnei's mother managed to use some influence with the judge and get custody of all three children. What followed was eight years of horrifying abuse as mother Louella went through a series of increasingly insane husbands, eight in all. The Dubois family, who'd fostered Whitnei, managed to persuade Louella to let them have the girl for some of the time, but in the end she was always dragged back to her mother and her stream of partners. The last of these abused and raped Whitnei and her older sister Taylor for almost three years until finally he snapped and gave Taylor a serious beating. At that point Las Vegas Social Services got involved, and when Louella chose her violent husband over her children the Dubois family managed to bring both ten-year-old Whitnei and Taylor back to Louisiana and adopt them. It was too late for Whitnei though – she was already profoundly damaged by her early life. As she struggled through high school she continually changed styles and even personalities.[v] At 17 she dropped out of school and at 18 she left home and got a job in a fast food restaurant. Then, as often tragically happens, she fell into the same self-destructive behavior she'd seen from her mother. She moved in with a boyfriend who could supply her with pills and in 2001 got arrested when their home was raided for drugs. At this point she had maybe her last chance to break free of her mother's legacy; she found she was pregnant and the police let her go. Instead of returning to her boyfriend's house she moved back in at the Dubois home.

Looking after a baby in a decent, stable home was exactly the thing that might have sorted Whitnei out, but life had another dose of bad luck for her. The birth was difficult and she needed a caesarian, which then got infected. To cope with the pain she was prescribed some powerful analgesics, much stronger than the recreational pills she'd been playing around with, and when the prescription ran out she quickly got sucked deeper into the local drug scene. At first she tried to stay clean at home for her daughter's sake but it didn't take long for her to mess up and lose custody of the child. Then the father was released from jail and Whitnei moved back in with him; that made things even worse. The relationship was a turbulent one, too much like Louella's had been; for a while Whitnei stayed in a women's shelter, but got asked to leave because she wouldn't stop seeing him. It all hit bottom when she started using crack. Her adopted sister Brittney Jones tried to get her into rehab but instead Whitnei was arrested again; the police had an outstanding warrant against her for writing bad checks. This time she spent a month in jail. When she was released Brittney took her in again and tried to get her cleaned up, and at first it seemed to be working. Then Whitnei found a new boyfriend – another druggie. She moved in with him and everything Brittney had achieved was instantly undone. In early May 2007 Whitnei and her new man had a fight and he threw her out. For a few days she bounced around between various places where she could find a bed for the night. Late on May 10 she visited her brother Mike, then went to her mother's house briefly where she's believed to have stolen some prescription pills.[vi] She returned to Mike's house late at night then slipped out again while he was asleep. Finally she headed off to Frankie Richard's house. Richard says she didn't stay long and left early in the morning of May 11. That was the last anyone remembers seeing her alive.

She wasn't gone for long. On May 12 the nude body of a woman was found dumped at an intersection, three miles south of Jennings and only a thousand yards from where Ernestine Daniels had been discovered two years earlier. There was a difference this time; the three previous corpses had all been found in water but this one had been discarded in the middle of a dirt track right where it joined the intersection of Bobby Road and Earl Duhon Road. These roads aren't busy, unlike the state highways that carry a lot of long-distance trucks, but even so there was no attempt at concealment. The body was already slightly decomposed, despite the short time since she'd vanished, and the sheriff told the press that she hadn't died where she'd been dumped. She was found at 7:30 in the morning, just an hour after sunrise, so it's most probable the killer dropped her at the intersection sometime the previous night.

Because the corpse wasn't as badly deteriorated as the other three there were hopes that more evidence could be collected from it. It didn't take long to identify it as Whitnei from fingerprint records – hers were on file after her arrests for drug use and forging checks – but there weren't any hints about what had killed her. There were high levels of alcohol and cocaine in her system, which wasn't a surprise given her lifestyle, but no sign of any forensic clues to what had happened.

Chapter 3: The Peak Of The Series

LaConia Shontell Brown, known as Muggy, was another well-known member of the Jennings vice scene. She was popular with her social circle, which included plenty of the local dealers and prostitutes, but there was a darker side to her personality. As well as selling herself Brown also procured younger girls, got them high on drugs then hired them out to customers. In December 2005 she and Lawrence Nixon, who'd been held for Loretta Chaisson's murder, were arrested for conspiracy to rape a minor.

On the evening of May 28, 2008 Muggy was at her grandmother's home in south Jennings. About 8pm she filled a bag with dirty clothes and told her grandmother she was going out to do some laundry. Bessie Brown was puzzled at this because she had a washing machine in the house, but she didn't say anything. Muggy came and went as she pleased, and besides she'd been nervous and jumpy the past few days. If she wanted to go to the laundromat she was going to go.

She didn't come back.

Around 2am in the morning on May 29 a police officer driving down Racca Road, just southeast of Jennings, saw something sprawled in the headlight beams. Racca Road is a dirt track off Prairie 2-26B and it's less than 400 yards long; the only place it leads is the sheriff's office shooting ranges. Dumped right at the start of the first range was the corpse of a woman. At first the officer thought the victim was wearing a pink tank top and white capri pants. In fact the top was white too; it had been stained with blood that had poured from a slit throat, then the gore had been diluted with some other liquid. One sniff was enough to tell what that had been – the body stank of bleach.

The four previous corpses had started to decompose by the time they were found, but Muggy's had barely even lost its body heat. This should have been a chance to start making progress with forensics, but the bleach that soaked the skin and clothes would have seared away a lot of potential clues. Bleach works by breaking down chemical bonds and it's especially effective on organic substances like blood or hair. It can even break down the DNA molecules needed to get a genetic fingerprint (although it's not quite as effective at that as many people think it is). The cause of death was obvious though – the gaping wound across the throat. That matched the only other body where cause of death had been confirmed, Ernestine Daniels.

By 8:30 that morning police were searching a house on Spencer Street, one street over from Bessie Brown's home. The Sheriff's Office Forensic Investigation Unit from neighboring Calcasieu Parish was called in as well, bringing more advanced forensic gear than the Jefferson Davis sheriff's office had. Muggy had known the occupant of the house and as soon as neighbors saw the police there they called her sister Gail. That was the first warning they had, but soon after they heard that another dead woman had been found.

It didn't take long to identify the body as Muggy's. Police made an initial ID from her tattoos, then confirmed it by checking dental and medical records. Apart from the identification they didn't get a lot from it though. Once again the body showed high levels of alcohol and cocaine. Like the first two victims – but unlike the third and fourth – Muggy had still been dressed when she was found. Like all the victims she was missing her shoes. That fact helped to fuel speculation about a serial killer, with some in the sheriff's office believing the killer had taken the women's footwear to satisfy a fetish. There's another explanation however, and it's a lot more mundane. All the killings took place when the weather was warm and at least some of them were wearing light footwear. The easiest way to drag a body is to catch hold of it under the armpits, and shoes – especially light ones like flip flops – often get knocked off as the feet trail along the ground. Hauling the dead women in our out of a vehicle would also be likely to remove their footwear. If the killer was aware of how often that happens they might even have taken them off and ditched them immediately just to cut the risk of having them fall off unnoticed and leave a clue.

- X -

Crystal Shay Benoit Zeno was another girl with a troubled history. In February 2003, aged 19, she'd married 47-year-old Elmer Ray Harrison; eighteen months later he was dead. Not long after she married again, to Stanley Lee Zeno. Her family lived in Lake Arthur and she worked in the Sonic Burger restaurant there until May 2008, when she relocated to Jennings with her young daughter Ananey Paige and moved in with Brittney Gary. Lake Arthur was only ten miles south and she still got back there often enough – she visited Sonic Burger on August 27. On August 29 she was back in Jennings and that afternoon she called the sheriff's office from the Phillips 66 gas station on West Plaquemine Street. By the time a patrol car reached the gas station she was gone.

On September 11 a group of hunters found a badly decomposed female body in a strip of woods that runs close to Highway 1126, a mile south of where Muggy's corpse had been dumped in May. The remains were unidentifiable but from the description released the suspicion was that it was Shay Benoit. Like three of the five other victims no cause of death could be determined but high levels of alcohol and cocaine were again found. Samples were taken for DNA testing and the body rested in Matthews and Son Funeral Home, the local undertakers, while the family and town waited for the results. On November 9 it was confirmed that the body was Shay, and the preliminary finding was that she'd been a victim of homicide.

Not long after the discovery of the corpse a Lafayette man called the Jefferson Davis DA's office with some information. He said he'd seen three African-American men he recognized leaving the wood where Shay had been dumped. They were Eugene Ivory, Ervin Mouton and Ricardo Williams. What got the DA's attention was that Ivory was a known friend of Frankie Richard, whose name kept appearing in the investigation. Mouton had also been looked at as a suspect in the killing of Kristen Lopez.

- X -

Another name that kept surfacing was Teresa
Gary. A close friend and alleged criminal
accomplice of Richard, she was also deeply
involved with the drug scene and sometimes
stayed at a notorious crack hangout on South
Andrew Street. She knew or was related to all six
of the victims - Kristen Lopez was her niece -
and had worked with a couple of them in fast
food restaurants. Her 17-year-old daughter
Brittney had been Muggy Brown's best friend.
Of course that meant young Brittney had plenty
of exposure to the dark underside of life in
Jennings and slowly she was dragged into it too.
A tiny, slightly chubby girl – she was only 5 feet
tall – she spent a lot of time hanging out with
women much older than herself who were
deeply involved in drugs and prostitution.
Sometime in early 2008 the family moved to
Texas for a few months, and returned to
Jennings around October 30. Brittney doesn't
seem to have been completely happy about that;
within days she told her mother, "You don't
know who you can trust anymore. They can be
your friend. You just never know."

If Brittney was trying to guess who was killing her friends, she got it wrong. On November 2 she dropped by the crack den on Andrews Street to return a jacket she'd borrowed, then walked six blocks north. Around 5:30pm she was recorded by a CCTV camera buying cell phone credit at the Family Dollar store on West Plaquemine Street, just across the intersection from the Phillips 66 where Shay Benoit had made her last phone call. The footage shows her paying for her purchases and walking out the store towards the gas station. That's the last image of her alive – all the gas station's cameras apparently weren't working that day.[vii] Right after that she stopped answering her cell phone. Next evening Teresa reported her missing.

At first the Jennings police treated it as a simple missing person case. Normally that wouldn't be unreasonable. Teenagers, especially from troubled families – and Brittney's definitely qualified – run away a lot. Given the fact she was linked to six women who had vanished then turned up dead it could be argued that the city cops should have made different assumptions in this case. The parish sheriff's office seems to have leaned more in that direction and started their own investigation,[viii] but in public they denied any connection.

On November 15 a search party organized by Brittney's uncle Butch found her decomposing body dumped beside a dirt track in the rice fields out west of the town. They immediately called the local police, who secured the scene and, for the first time, called in the FBI. Brittney's aunt later revealed that the cause of death was listed as asphyxiation.

- X -

On December 18 Sheriff Edwards announced the formation of a special task force to investigate the killings. Officially known as a Multi Agency Investigative Team, it was funded by $250,000 from the state of Louisiana and brought in more than a dozen separate agencies. These included the sheriff's offices of neighboring parishes, state agencies and the FBI. With the technical resources the task force could call on there was a much better chance of finding a critical piece of evidence that could break the case open. But it should have been done much earlier. By the time it was set up the cycle of death was drawing to a close; there was only one more death to come.

- X -

Necole Guillory was one of the most notorious prostitutes in town, with a long and varied list of crimes against her name. She was into almost everything – theft and drugs were reliable earners – and she could take care of herself. In 2006, when a client gave her a hard time, she battered him with a sledgehammer handle.[ix] Mysteriously, for someone who'd been arrested so much, she was rarely if ever punished. In fact the DA's office seemed very reluctant to press charges and most indictments were quickly dropped for lack of public interest. To anyone familiar with how law enforcement works this says one thing – police informer.

Informers are an essential tool for investigators and clearance rates would be a lot lower without them, but running them can be a dirty business. It's always hard to know where to draw the line, and which of the snitch's own crimes should be overlooked in exchange for information about bigger fish. Plenty of careers have come to an end because cops got it wrong.

Obviously at least somebody in the sheriff's office wasn't willing to give Guillory unlimited rope, because her luck ran out in January 2007; she was convicted of possessing crack cocaine and spent 20 months in the parish jail. Released on probation, she quickly showed that she was far from a reformed character. Within a few weeks there was a warrant out for her arrest on parole violation charges. There were also whispers of other threats to her; one of her fellow prostitutes told the murder task force that Guillory could be the next victim. Guillory herself seems to have picked up something. She told her mother she would be dead before her 27th birthday, and sent her four children off to live with relatives. Her fears seemed to be well placed. She was last seen alive on August 16, getting into an unidentified car on Doyle Street; on August 19 her mother went to the police and reported that Necole had been missing for three days.

She wasn't missing for long. Just over an hour later her body was found near a highway bridge on I-10, dumped in an overgrown ballpark just over the county line in Acadia Parish. As with Brittney Gary's body the FBI were called in to the scene, but there wasn't much to go on; the corpse had been partly stripped and was only wearing a white blouse, but no cause of death could be found. Again, toxicology reports showed high levels of alcohol and cocaine in Necole's system.

Guillory was wild and headstrong, but in many ways she was a lot less dysfunctional than other victims. She paid a lot of attention to her personal appearance, usually dressing in a spotless white blouse like the one she was wearing when she died. She was rarely seen without a hairbrush in her hand and groomed her long dark hair constantly. Even when walking she'd have her head to one side as she worked the brush in long, steady strokes. That habit made her easy to recognize at a distance. When her killer targeted her she would have been easy to spot.

Chapter 4: Serial Killer?

Because the killings were spaced out and irregular, with long gaps in the series, it was a while before people started to connect them with each other. After all street prostitutes who're involved with drugs (which is most of them) run appalling risks. They hang around quiet streets at night. They get into cars with strangers. They're at risk from aggressive clients and very vulnerable to muggers or cruising predators. When one gets killed it's a tragedy – although too many people still take a judgmental attitude and act as if they've somehow earned it – but not a surprise. As the death toll mounted many started to wonder if they were connected, and long before Necole Guillory died the common belief was that a serial killer was at work in Jefferson Davis Parish.

Serial killers fascinate a lot of people. Movies about real-life cases pull in huge audiences and books on them regularly become bestsellers. Fictional ones can be even more of a draw – Hannibal Lecter is more anti-hero than villain, a cultured genius who's far more sympathetic than many of his victims. The charm goes away when a real serial killer is stalking your neighborhood though. These criminals tend to prey on a particular type of victim and for anyone who falls into that group there's a constant nagging anxiety – "Will I be next?" Everyone else can't afford to get complacent either; the killer might just decide to change the rules. English murderer Peter Sutcliffe – the Yorkshire Ripper – started out killing prostitutes. He claimed to have reasons for that, sometimes saying that one had cheated him out of £10, or occasionally going for the old standby "God told me to do it." His fifth victim wasn't a sex worker and after that, while he kept attacking streetwalkers, he seems to have decided that any woman would do as a target. In fact before he graduated to killing he'd already seriously injured four women. Three of them were hookers, but the fourth was a 14-year-old schoolgirl. Whoever was killing women in Jefferson Davis Parish was choosing victims from a fairly small pool centered in south Jennings, but there was no guarantee they wouldn't widen their horizons. Any woman in the parish could be next.

After Shay Benoit's body was discovered in September 2008 parish sheriff Ricky Edwards held a press conference to discuss the situation. Under intense questioning from reporters he pointed out that of the six deaths in the apparent series only three – Daniels, Brown and Benoit – were definitely homicides. Edwards acknowledged the possibility of a serial killer but in a slightly baffling statement introduced the idea of a "serial dumper." When a journalist asked him what that meant Edwards replied, "I really don't know. That's terminology I guess we're making up."[x] That was definitely true. Edwards went on to link the idea to someone who was involved in a series of fatal overdoses and then dumped the bodies to avoid a drug arrest. It was at least possible, but the odds of the same person being involved in that many accidental ODs were slim and if they weren't accidental serial murder was back on the agenda.

Edwards was technically correct to say that only three of the deaths to that point were definite homicides, but that didn't mean much in reality. Because of the way the bodies had been dumped it was almost certain that they all were and, given that fact, there were enough similarities to make a serial killer a very real possibility. Serial killers tend to choose their victims from one ethnic group – usually their own – but that's not always the case. If another selection factor is strong enough to override ethnicity the result can be a multi-racial victim group. It would even make sense to argue that there were two separate killers at work; both black victims had had their throats cut, but none of the white ones appeared to have.

All the victims hung out in south Jennings and around the cheap motels that fringe the town. Some of them sold sex at truck stops, where the 18-wheelers that rumble endlessly to and fro along Interstate 10 pull in so the drivers can eat or sleep. Serial killers are often transient and it isn't just truckers who stop there, so there was a possibility that the killer wasn't from the area and was picking up victims along I-10. It was even suggested that the long gaps between murders – almost two years between Daniels and Lopez, more than a year between Dubois and Brown – could indicate the perpetrator was a serviceman who had been deployed abroad twice. Set against that, at least one behavioral profiler believed that if a single killer was responsible the likely culprit would be a white male aged from 28 to 34 years old, unskilled, a high school dropout and with no military service.[xi]

These days the public knows what a serial killer is and when a string of apparently similar unsolved murders happens in an area it's the obvious conclusion to draw. There were also some very good arguments *against* this being the work of a serial killer, though. The USA has far more serial killers than any other nation, so the world's leading experts on the subject are, without any doubt, the FBI's Behavioral Analysis Unit. According to their research serial killers almost always murder strangers; there's very rarely an obvious link between the offender and the victims. There's also usually no link between the victims, and when it came to the Jeff Davis Eight nothing could be further from the truth – the victims were very closely linked indeed. They all knew each other, they all did the same things in the same places and some of them were even blood relatives. Of course they mostly had something else in common; apart from Ernestine Daniels they were all friends of Frankie Richard.

Chapter 5: Number One Suspect

Frankie Richard was born sometime around 1956 to 19-year-old Jeanette LeBlanc. After leaving school Richard – he pronounces it *Ree-shar*, in the French style – worked on rigs in the Gulf oil fields for a while, then came back to Jennings and opened the first in a string of strip clubs he used to run along I-10. By the early 2000s he had drifted into the drug scene in South Jennings; by his own admission he was addicted to crack. He wasn't just a user though. Along with his mother he was involved in the supply side too, doing a steady business in prescription painkillers. That's probably what brought him into contact with the murdered women. In fact if he was a dealer the only surprise is that he had links to only seven of the victims, not all eight.

Richard had already gone through routine interviews because he'd been seen with Loretta Chaisson in the days before she vanished, but the first time he was seriously linked to the killings was after the death of Kristen Lopez. He admitted that she'd been at his motel room shortly before she disappeared but claimed she had then left in the truck with Connie Siler and Tracee Chaisson. Then, two days after Lopez was found, Siler was arrested for check fraud. Because police knew Lopez often rode in the truck with her, and she had been with Lopez around the time she was last seen alive, she was questioned about the visit to Richard at the Budget Inn on March 6. She backed up what Richard had said – the three women had left the Budget Inn after Richard told them to get out his room. Tracee Chaisson also repeated this story – at first. Then, in her second interrogation, she broke down and said something very different. In tears Chaisson described how Richard and his niece, Hannah Conner, had lost their tempers with Lopez during a frenzied drug session. They'd given her a severe beating on a levee beside the Petitjean Canal, then drowned her. Lopez had been found in the canal, which made Chaisson's story credible. Months later it was backed up by a statement from an inmate in the parish lockup who said Conner, after taking crack, had told her she and Richard had killed Lopez.

There were some inconsistencies. Chaisson said the killing had happened on the outskirts of Jennings, but Lopez was found twelve miles to the southwest. Two inmates – the woman who'd reported Conner's confession and another one – had an answer for that. They told investigators that Richard had stuffed the corpse into a barrel and hauled it to the dump site in the back of a truck. The truck, they said, had then been bought by a friend of Richard who'd washed it to get rid of any traces of Lopez's DNA. Worryingly, the friend was a police officer; one of the inmates thought he was called Mr. Warren.

It later came out that Chaisson had told a similar story about the death of Shay Dubois; a woman told a Jeff Davis police sergeant that Chaisson had described the murder to her. A drug party had been going on, she said, when Richard started making sexual advances to Dubois. She'd turned him down and he got aggressive. Dubois fought back, until Richard knocked her down, got on top of her and started punching. Conner then held the girl's head underwater until she drowned.[xii] In fact these stories are more than similar – they're practically identical. It's possible that Richard and Conner killed two (or more) girls in exactly the same way, but it's just as likely that either Chaisson or the witness was mixed up about the victim's identity in one case. Either way, here was eyewitness testimony that Richard had killed one of the dead women. That made him a likely candidate for all of them, because he'd known seven of the victims and probably knew the eighth at least by sight.

Hannah Conner was picked up on May 15 and charged with the second-degree murder of Kristen Lopez.[xiii] Richard was already in the cells charged with a rape that had happened the day before; now the same charge of second-degree murder was laid on him as well. Sheriff Edwards announced that the two were also being investigated in connection with the other deaths, including Whitnei Dubois who had been found three days earlier. It soon became clear that Richard, at least, couldn't have been involved in all four deaths; Edwards found out he'd been in rehab when one of the victims disappeared. Then the case weakened further. Tracee Chaisson kept changing her story – four times, according to parish DA Michael Cassidy - and as that was the only real evidence the sheriff's office had they quickly ran out of reasons to hold Richard and Conner. Within days of the charges being laid they were withdrawn, and Conner was released. Chaisson had also been charged by this time; she was the one who'd reported Lopez missing and investigators thought she'd already known where the body was when she did it, so they'd charged her with being an accessory after the fact. Those charges were dropped, too. Richard stayed in jail over the rape charge, but was released in July when the alleged victim suddenly withdrew her story.

Lopez had been missing for twelve days before her body was found, and in the hot, humid climate that was long enough for the corpse to deteriorate badly. No cause of death had been determined but the autopsy did provide some information. There were no obvious signs of wounds to the scalp, and if she'd been badly beaten around the head some traces would probably have remained. There were also no fractures to the skull or ribs,[xiv] which usually occur if someone receives a life-threatening beating. That wasn't enough to rule Chaisson's story out completely, but it didn't really support it either. Richard had a long history of assaults behind him and was easily powerful enough to have battered Lopez to death if he'd wanted, and it's unlikely that if he'd attacked her in a drug-fueled rage he would have taken care not to break anything obvious.

After Lopez, the victim with the clearest connection to Richard is Whitnei Dubois. He admits to having been one of the last people to see her alive; in fact if he's telling the truth nobody apart from the killer saw her again after she walked out of his house early on May 10, 2007. If he *isn't* telling the truth… well, who knows? The problem is there aren't any other witnesses to corroborate his story, and there *is* testimony that he killed her.

Sometime before Brittney Ann Gary went to Texas early the next year she went round to Whitnei's sister's house, stood in the yard and yelled, "You know Uncle Frankie killed your sister?"

Chapter 6: The Cops

The Jefferson Davis Parish Sheriff's Office was founded in 1913, the year the parish itself was established. It's responsible for the usual range of law enforcement tasks as well as some called for by the landscape of the parish – a Marine Division and a livestock patrol, for example. Since the 1960s it's been headquartered in a boxy brown brick complex that takes up most of a block on East Plaquemine Road in Jennings. As well as offices there's the parish police jury and a 62-bed jail. Policing in Jennings itself is handled by the Jennings PD, who operate out of a smaller facility two blocks south at the corner of North Market Street and North Broadway, that also houses the City Court and fire station. Between the two it seems that law enforcement in the area should be pretty well covered, but in fact the local police have some serious trust issues with the community.

As far back as the 1970s there were rumors about local cops making some extra cash out of the drug trade. Then in 1990 two Jennings men robbed the sheriff's office and hauled off 300 pounds of marijuana from the evidence room. They were quickly caught, but told investigators they'd been helped by two accomplices. One of the men they named was Frankie Richard. The other was Ted Gary, the chief deputy sheriff. The burglars were convicted and no charges were brought against the alleged accomplices.

In 1992 Sheriff Dallas Cormier was arrested and charged with obstruction of justice. Among the crimes he was accused of were improper relations with inmates in the parish jail and misuse of public funds. The next year he pleaded guilty in federal court; by that time he'd been replaced as sheriff by Ricky Edwards Jr.

It didn't take long for Edwards to find himself
the subject of accusations, too. In 1996 a Hispanic
couple from out of state sued him in federal
court, claiming they had been caught in a traffic
stop carried out without probable cause. In 1997
NBC's *Dateline* show ran an hour-long special
alleging that the sheriff's office were illegally
targeting out of state cars for traffic stops, and
seizing vehicles under drug forfeiture laws
without adequate evidence. The show claimed
cops were exploiting Louisiana's often arcane
laws to raise funds; 20 per cent of the value of
any property they seized went to the judge, 20
per cent to the district attorney and the
remaining 60 per cent to the law enforcement
agency that made the seizure. Conveniently, the
burden of proof lay on the owner of the forfeited
property; to get it returned they had to prove
that their vehicle *wasn't* being used to transport
drugs, and it usually turns out that's a hard
thing to prove.

In 2003 eight female Jennings cops sued the city,
the mayor and the Police Department for a long
list of sexual harassment allegations that
included verbal abuse, inappropriate touching
and coerced sex acts. The complaint referred to
previous allegations of sexual discrimination
and harassment that had not been investigated,
indicating a long-standing problem in the
department.[xv]

- X -

Some of the allegations touched directly on the murders. The most serious of these was the issue of Connie Siler's truck. As the investigation into Kristen Lopez's death gained speed Siler had been locked up in the parish jail; her truck was in the pound after being recovered from a driveway where it had been abandoned. The truck was only a year old and Siler had paid close to $20,000 for it, but she couldn't meet the repayments and her bank was threatening to foreclose. Now, as well as the bad check charges that had put her in jail, she was being interviewed about the deaths of Lopez and the three previous victims. Her interrogator was Warren Gary, a detective who'd been with the Jeff Davis sheriff's office since July 1992 and was now the Chief Criminal Investigator. Allegedly Siler told him about her problems with the truck repayments and mentioned that she'd be interested in selling it. The policy in the sheriff's office is that they hold an impounded vehicle for ten days if the owner is in jail and nobody can pick it up. On March 29 2007, nine days after Siler had been arrested, Gary passed her a message through jail warden Terrie Guillory; her truck would be handed over to a wrecker's yard the next day, when the holding period expired. Siler passed a message back that she was still interested in selling it.[xvi] Next day she was released from jail and sold the Silverado to Gary for $8,748.90 – just over half its blue book value.

Siler used the money to make restitution for the bad checks she'd written and to pay off the outstanding loan; Gary had the truck washed and, three weeks later, sold it for $15,500 to a state trooper's ex-wife who, conveniently, was about to move to California. It was the purchase and resale that landed him in trouble with the state Board of Ethics, earning him a reprimand and a $10,000 fine, but according to claims by a female inmate at the parish jail there was a deeper motive behind the deal.

- X -

In December 2007 Sergeant Jessie Ewing, a detective with the Jennings PD, got word that two female inmates in the jail wanted to talk about the unsolved murders. They repeated Chaisson's claims about the murders of Lopez and Dubois, but what was more interesting were the allegations they made about the truck. They told Ewing that Frankie Richard and a senior investigator – "Mr. Warren," obviously Warren Gary – had conspired to get the truck out of the way before it could be examined for evidence in the Lopez case; one of the inmates said Hannah Conner had told her they knew the truck might contain traces of DNA from Lopez, so they arranged for Gary to buy it. He then washed it at a car wash in town and sold it on as quickly as he could. Even if the truck could now be examined, anything that was found would be tainted by the changes of ownership. According to the inmate Gary had done this because he was a close friend of Richard.[xvii] It was a direct allegation of collusion between Richard and a senior member of the sheriff's office, with the aim of covering up Richard's involvement in at least one homicide.

Sheriff Ricky Edwards later claimed that the truck deal had been unethical but there had been no intention to interfere with the case; at that time, he said, nobody had even known it was involved. Paula Guillory, a sheriff's office detective, disagreed; they already knew the truck had probably been involved in the murder, she told an investigative journalist. All the same Guillory's own husband, jail warden Terrie, was making his own contribution to muddying the waters. He provided an alibi for Hannah Conner, claiming that her movements round the time Lopez died were down to her job for a cable company. It was a day job and the movements in question had been at night, so the alibi wasn't exactly solid, but it was enough to help get the charges against Conner dropped.

Sergeant Ewing had distrusted some of his fellow cops for a while, but the allegations in his interview tapes were something else. This wasn't just a feeling that some officers liked to play fast and loose with the rules; he had two people claiming that a senior detective had conspired with a notorious drug dealer to cover up at least one murder. Not surprisingly he had the idea that if he passed his tapes up the chain they were likely to disappear. Instead he handed copies to Kirk Menard, a private investigator, to pass on to the FBI office in Lake Charles.

Incredibly, the FBI didn't investigate the allegations against Gary. Instead they passed the tapes back to the MAIT task force – which was dominated by the Jeff Davis Sheriff's Office. Not long after, the parish DA charged Ewing with malfeasance in office and sexual misconduct with one of the inmates who'd given him his information, who was now claiming he had touched the other inmate inappropriately during the interview. That charge was dropped, probably because the interview tapes didn't back it up. Ewing himself says that one of the women pulled her shirt up and exposed her breasts suggestively during an interview. Suspicious, Kirk Menard managed to interview the cellmates of the two women Ewing had spoken to. They claimed they'd overheard Ewing's witnesses discussing framing him in exchange for getting released.[xviii] That could only have worked if someone senior had offered them a deal. In any case the sexual misconduct charge collapsed, but the DA still managed to end Ewing's 20-year police career on the basis of the malfeasance charges. Meanwhile Warren Gary was promoted and moved to a new job – running the evidence room.

- X -

The evidence room at the sheriff's office didn't seem to have much luck. Paula Guillory was suspended on July 7, 2009 – and later terminated – for stealing $3,791 in cash that was being held as evidence in a drugs case. The suspects in the case were Jeanette LeBlanc, her daughter Tabatha Crochet and her son – Frankie Richard. Until she was dismissed Guillory was a member of the task force investigating the killings – and her husband Terrie was Necole Guillory's cousin. In 2013 former Jennings police chief Johnny Lassiter, who'd also been on the task force, was convicted of stealing cash and a huge quantity of drugs from the evidence room.

The sacking of Paula Guillory raises multiple questions. On June 4, 2009 she took part in a raid on the home where Richard lived with his extended family. The target was a diverse criminal enterprise allegedly run by Richard, his mother and Teresa Gary, Brittney's mother. As well as drugs the gang was accused of masterminding the theft of guns, jewelry and collectible coins from Jennings homes. Guillory, working with Warren Gary, helped catalog the evidence seized during the raid. She claims she realized nearly $4,000 was missing and notified her superiors, but was immediately suspended by Sheriff Edwards without being given a chance to tell her side of the story. She offered to take a polygraph test, she says, but was refused.

By Guillory's account she was an honest, hard-working cop who was fired for trying to do the right thing, and the involvement of Warren Gary gives her story a certain credibility – after the truck incident there's no denying that he was willing to interfere with evidence. Comments from fellow detectives paint a different picture though. One of them, Derrick Miller, accused her of leaking information about the murders and claimed that since she was hired there had been a number of thefts from the office. Other allegations link her closely to the vice business in the town and Miller claimed it was widely known that one of her daughters was a drug user. Guillory had constant financial problems, to the point where her utilities were sometimes cut off, but a month after the cash from the raid went missing she had landscaping work done in her yard.[xix] The allegations against her were taken seriously enough that an external agency – Vermilion Parish Sheriff's Office – was asked to investigate, so it's hard to write it off as an internal whitewash.

- X -

Ex-husband Terrie Guillory had had his share of critics, too. He's been accused of pimping out female inmates in the jail when he was warder there, including his cousin Necole. Multiple witnesses also say Paula and Terrie visited Richard's home and the crack den on South Andrew Street, both locations linked to all the victims. Paula had legitimate reasons for visiting these places – she was on the task force, after all – but it's harder to explain why Terrie would have gone along. His job was running the jail, not investigating murders. Mike Dubois, Shay's brother, says Terrie Guillory was also pulling in and interrogating potential witnesses. That's odd enough; again, it wasn't his job. What's even stranger is that most of his questions seemed to be about himself, and whether any of the street girls had mentioned meeting him.[xx]

- X -

Since 2008 the task force has collected hundreds
of pages of witness statements and, over and
over again, witnesses have told investigators
that some of the victims were frightened of the
police, or involved with the sheriff's office in
other ways. Days before she died Muggy Brown
told her sister she was helping a cop investigate
a murder, but she was telling others that three
police officers were planning to kill her. Necole
Guillory often said that cops were behind the
murders; her mother begged her to write down
what she knew but she refused, saying it would
put the rest of the family in danger.

In November 2008 three witnesses who spoke to
the task force named the same cop in a single
day of interviews. They claimed that Danny
Barry, who had joined the sheriff's office in 1998,
used to cruise round the south side of town with
his wife, trying to pick up women. If they could
persuade one to get in the car they'd give her a
spiked drink then take her back to the trailer
where they lived. According to one of the
witnesses there was a room in the trailer fitted
out with bondage gear, including chains. The
task force interviewed Barry once, in February
2009, and none of the allegations against him
were brought up. He died in 2010.[xxi]

- X -

When Brittney Gary was found, the search party member who discovered her body immediately called 911 and the sheriff's office came out to secure the crime scene. When they arrived he says he handed one of the detectives a medallion he'd found near the body. Later the searcher returned to the scene with Mike Dubois, Whitnei's brother, to show him where the body was found. They discovered two evidence bags that had been left beside the road. On handing them in to the sheriff's office he says he was told to leave town and never come back.[xxii]
There's also plenty more evidence of deep links between the local police and Frankie Richard. In 2012 two women went to the task force to pass on information linking Frankie Richard to the murders. A senior investigator told them, "Don't worry about Frankie. He works for me."[xxiii]

- X -

Ethan Brown believes the sheriff's office and Jennings PD are so riddled with corruption that they're an obstacle to solving the case, not an asset. The new sheriff, Ivy Woods – who was elected in 2011 at least partly because he promised to solve the murders – acknowledges that there were problems in the past, but insists local law enforcement is now moving in the right direction. If the sheriff's office isn't corrupt, however, either Jefferson Davis Parish has unusually cunning murderers or the cops are well-meaning but stunningly incompetent. It's bad enough that eight women have been killed by a perpetrator who's still at large – but since Loretta Chaisson was found in the canal there have been *nine* other unsolved murders in the area. According to the FBI the parish has one of the lowest homicide clearance rates in the entire USA. Nationally, 64 per cent of homicides are solved. In Jeff Davis it's less than seven per cent.

Chapter 7: Parallel Investigations

For whatever reason it's obvious that law enforcement in Jefferson Davis Parish have a very poor record in solving homicide cases. By the time Shay Benoit died a lot of the locals, and especially the families of the victims, had pretty much given up hope of the police getting to the bottom of the killings. Determined to find someone who could do better, two of the families (their identities haven't been revealed) started looking for a private detective. On October 31, 2008, just two days before Brittney Gary disappeared, they hired Kirk Menard to investigate for them. When he took the job Menard spoke to a profiler he knew, and who he would later bring in to do a geographical study of the case. The profiler scanned the file briefly and warned Menard that there would be another death very soon.

- X -

A lot of private investigators have a law enforcement or even intelligence background. Kirk Menard didn't. What he did have was fourteen years' experience of looking into often complex incidents, starting out with investigating accidents in the oil and gas industry as an HSE coordinator for BP's Gulf operations.[xxiv] At the end of the day it doesn't matter much what you're investigating; the basic skills are the same. What's needed is an ability to collect information, piece it together and work out what's important. Menard had a talent for that. He soon diversified from the energy industry into covert surveillance, medical malpractice, missing persons, insurance fraud and a lot of other fields. By 2008 he was running his own agency, Menard Investigative Services LLC, and was an approved instructor for Louisiana's licensed private investigator course. He was also a Jennings native and understood the dynamics of life in the town.

In fact the case had touched Menard's life twice already. When Sergeant Ewing found evidence of law enforcement involvement that he couldn't entrust to his colleagues it was Menard he passed it to for delivery to the FBI. By the time the investigator was hired he was already well aware that there were questions about several people in the sheriff's office and Jennings PD. There was a more personal connection, too. When Muggy Brown and Lawrence Nixon were arrested for rape and conspiracy in December 2005 their victim was Menards's teenage daughter.

- X -

Menard had been following the pattern of dumpings and figured the best chance of catching the killer was to find him with a body in his truck. Sooner than he'd planned he had the chance to put his theory to the test. On November 2 Brittney Gary was reported missing and search parties went out. It's unlikely Menard thought there was any hope of finding her alive; all the evidence suggested the victims were being killed almost immediately. Even if Sheriff Edwards was saying Brittney was just a teenage runaway nobody else in the parish believed it and the assumption was she'd become victim number 7. When her uncle started organizing search parties he did the sensible thing and concentrated on areas similar to where the previous bodies had been dumped – canals, ditches and back roads. The searches were being carried out by townspeople, of course, and people talk. Most likely everyone in Jennings knew what areas had been searched. Many would have seen the teams at work; others would have listened to them talk as they relaxed with a beer after a long, hard day turning over the countryside.

Since *CSI: Crime Scene Investigation* first went on the air in 2000 real-life investigators are encountering a lot more crimes where perpetrators take precautions to limit physical evidence. Rape victims have reported being forced to shower after the attack, or wash themselves with bleach. Blackmailers seal envelopes with adhesive tape instead of licking them. Of course it works both ways; people have been caught because their adhesive tape picked up fingerprints, skin cells and even hair. One British rapist used tips gained from *CSI* and made his victims wipe themselves down with towels. He was jailed "at Her Majesty's pleasure" – in other words, indefinitely - after raping a woman who, unknown to him, was a fellow *CSI* fan; locked in the back of his car, she pulled out some of her own hair and spat on the seat.[xxv]

Menard believed that at least some of the Jeff Davis killings showed some degree of forensic awareness. Dumping bodies in water is a good way to remove physical evidence, especially if the water is warm and full of catfish and alligators. More than a couple of days outside in hot, humid weather will also get rid of a lot of traces. In the one case where the killer seemed to have wanted the body found quickly – Muggy Brown – it had been soaked with bleach. If he wanted Brittney's remains to weather for a few days, Menard reasoned, the simplest way would be to dump her somewhere that had already been searched; that narrowed down the possibilities. As for the likely time of dumping, it would probably be during darkness. Few of the roads in the parish are exactly busy, but it is agricultural land and during the day there would be farmers going about their business. If whoever had taken Brittney planned to dump her body the best chance of catching him in the act would be in a previously searched area at night.

- X -